Sarah M. Sweetser, Mary E Sweetser

Heart And Hand Work

Sarah M. Sweetser, Mary E Sweetser

Heart And Hand Work

ISBN/EAN: 9783744733861

Printed in Europe, USA, Canada, Australia, Japan

Cover: Foto ©Thomas Meinert / pixelio.de

More available books at **www.hansebooks.com**

HEART

AND

HAND WORK

BY THE COMPILERS OF "TRACING FOOTPRINTS"

D. LOTHROP & CO., PUBLISHERS, BOSTON.

PRINTED BY GUNN, BLISS & CO., 31 HAWLEY ST., BOSTON.

"*Each day's work comes to us wrapped in mystery which no human wisdom can explain or tell what in its completeness it will be when finished. There is, then, something brave and noble in the very act of hopefully accepting it, with whatever it brings of toil or pleasure, of light duties or burdens heavy to be borne, believing according to the day so shall our strength be.*"

"*Write it on your heart that every day is the best day in the year.*"

"WHAT are we set on earth for? Say, to toil;
Nor seek to leave thy tending of the vines,
For all the heat o' the day, till it declines,
And death's mild curfew shall from work assoil.
God did anoint thee with his odorous oil,
To wrestle, not to reign; and He assigns
All thy tears over, like pure crystallines,
For younger fellow-workers of the soil
To wear for amulets. So others shall
Take patience, labour, to their heart and hand,
From thy hand, and thy heart, and thy brave cheer,
And God's grace fructify through thee to all.
The least flower, with a brimming cup, may stand,
And share its dew-drop with another near."

"'What shall I do to gain eternal life?'
      Discharge aright
The simple dues with which each day is rife, —
      Yea, with thy might.
Ere perfect scheme of action thou devise
      Will life be fled;
While he who ever acts as conscience cries,
      Shall live, though dead."

"O TRIFLING task so often done,
  Yet ever to be done anew!
O cares which come with every sun,
  Morn after morn, the long years through!
    We sink beneath their paltry sway —
    The irksome calls of every day.

"The restless sense of wasted power,
  The tiresome sound of little things,
Are hard to bear, as hour by hour
  Its tedious iteration brings;
    Who shall evade or who delay
    The small demands of every day?

"Ah, more than martyr's aureole,
  And more than hero's heart of fire,
We need the humble strength of soul
  Which daily toils and ills require; —
    Sweet Patience! grant us, if you may,
    An added grace for every day!"

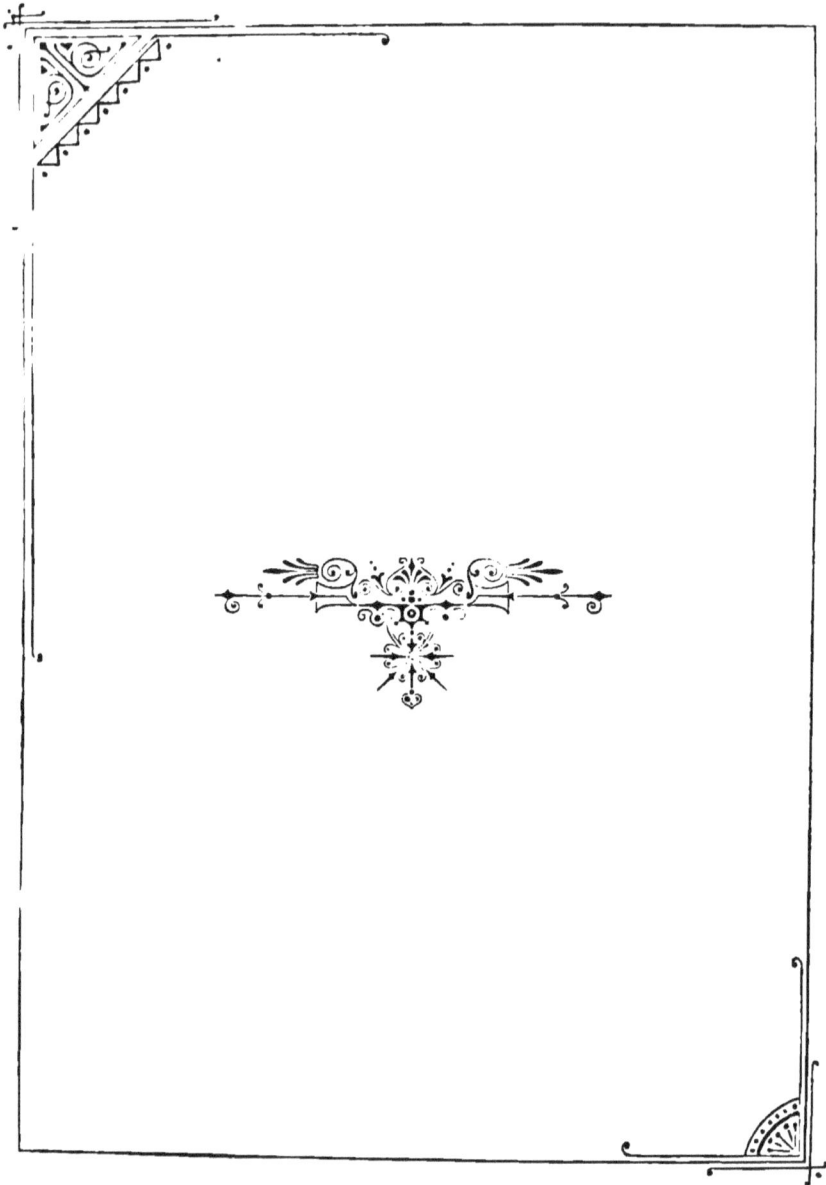

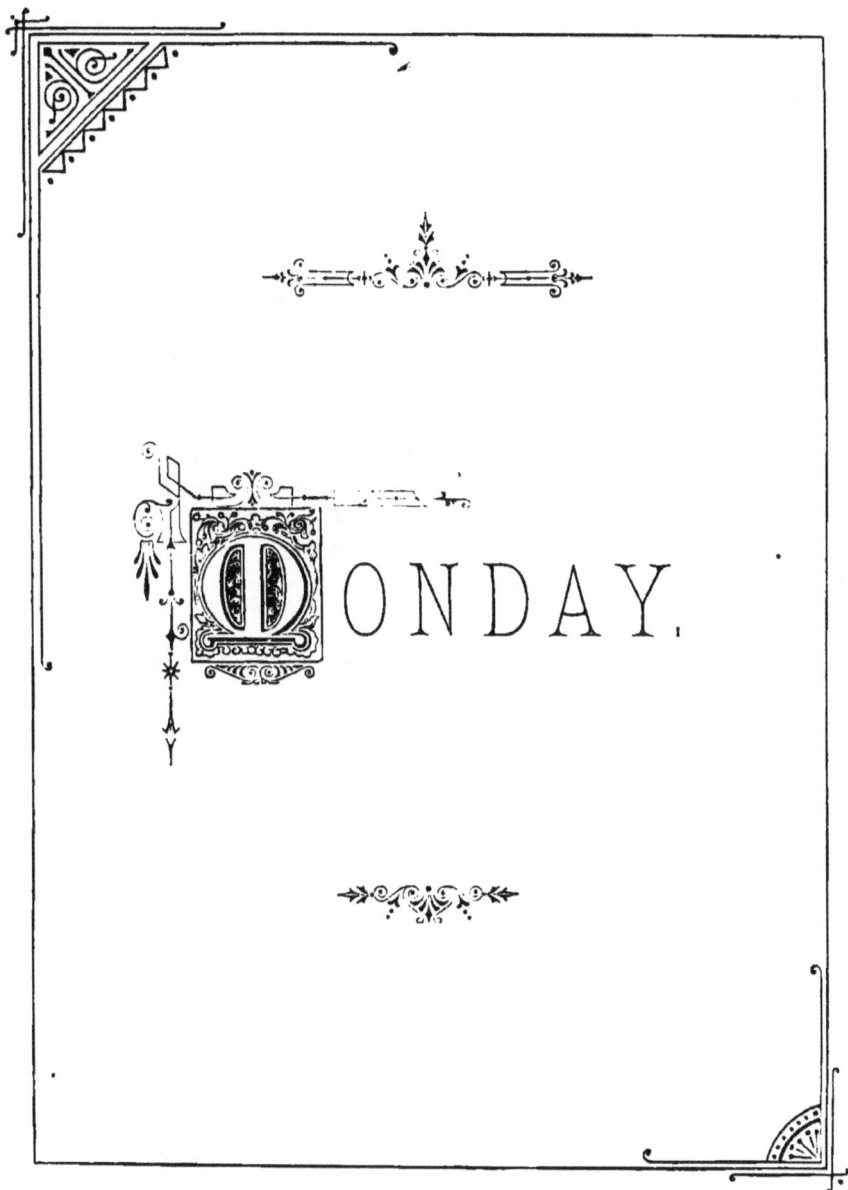

ONDAY.

WASH ye, make you clean; put away the evil of your doings from before mine eyes, cease to do evil.
— *Isaiah i. 16.*

And one of the elders answered, saying unto me, What are these which are arrayed in white robes? and whence came they? And I said unto him, Sir, thou knowest. And he said to me, These are they which came out of great tribulation, and have washed their robes, and made them white in the blood of the Lamb. — *Rev. vii. 13, 14.*

The blood of Jesus Christ his Son cleanseth us from all sin.
— *I John i, 7.*

Now Joshua was clothed with filthy garments, and stood before the angel. And he answered and spake unto those that stood before him, saying, Take away the filthy garments from him. And unto him he said, Behold, I have caused thine iniquity to pass from thee, and I will clothe thee with change of raiment. — *Zech. iii. 3, 4.*

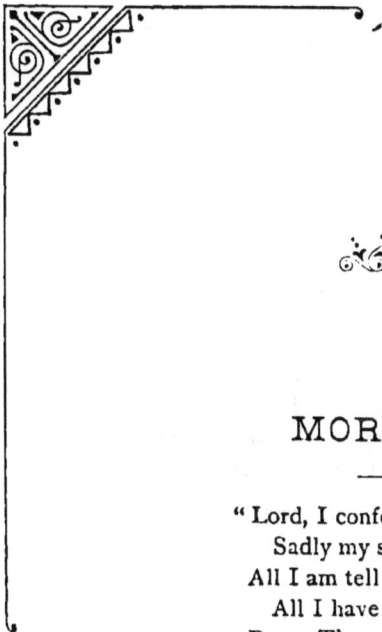

MORNING.

"Lord, I confess to Thee
 Sadly my sin;
All I am tell I Thee,
 All I have been.
Purge Thou my sin away,
Wash Thou my soul this day;
 Lord, make me clean."

DAY.

"My garments, travel-worn, and stained with dust,
Oft rent by briers and thorns that crowd my way,
Would fain be made, O Lord, my righteousness,
Spotless and *white* in heaven's unclouded ray."

"First in my tears I washed me, —
They could not make me clean :
A fountain then He showed me,
Strange until then unseen !
So close I'd lived beside it
For many weary years,
Yet passing by the fountain,
Had bathed me in my tears.
Oh, love, oh, grace, that showed it !
Revealed its *cleansing* power !
How could I choose but hasten
To meet Him from that hour."

"He came a leper all unclean and foul;
  He left as fresh as freshest infancy;
So come I to Thy feet, unclean in soul;
  So leave I, Lord, *cleansed* and restored by Thee.

"I touch Thee and am cured! No touch of mine
  Can render Thee impure, whatever
The foulness of the hand that touches Thine:
  Thee it defiles not, yet it *cleanses* me."

"Upon the mercy-seat
    The High Priest sits within;
  The blood is in His hand
    Which makes and keeps us *clean.*
With boldness let us now draw near;
That blood has banished every fear.

"Then to the Lamb once slain
    Be glory, praise, and power,
  Who died and lives again,
    Who liveth evermore:
Who loved and *washed* us in His blood,
Who made us kings and priests to God!"

EVENING.

"A moment from this outward life,
  Its service, self-denial, strife,
        I joyfully retreat;
My soul, through intercourse with Thee,
Strengthened, refreshed, and calmed shall be,
        Its scenes again to meet.

"How can it be that one so mean,
  A sinner, selfish, dark, unclean,
        Thus in the Holiest stands?
And in that light divinely pure
Which may no stain of sin endure,
        Lifts up rejoicing hands!

"Jesus! the answer Thou hast given!
  Thy death, Thy life, have opened heaven
        And all its joys to me;
Washed in Thy blood — oh! wondrous grace!
I'm holy as the Holy Place
        In which I worship Thee."

"And now, O Father! take
The heart I cast with humble faith on Thee,
And *cleanse* its depths from each impurity,
    For my Redeemer's sake."

TUESDAY.

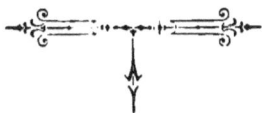

EVERY valley shall be filled, and every mountain and hill shall be brought low: and the crooked shall be made straight, and the rough ways shall be made smooth.—*Luke iii. 5.*

And I will bring the blind by a way that they knew not; I will lead them in paths that they have not known: I will make darkness light before them, and crooked things straight. These things will I do unto them, and not forsake them.—*Isaiah xlii. 16.*

The way of the righteous is made plain.—*Prov. xv. 19.*

MORNING.

"We praise Thee when our path is plain
And *smooth* beneath our feet;
But fain would learn to welcome pain,
And call the bitter sweet."

DAY.

"Mortal man and woman
  Go upon your travel!
Heaven assist the human
  Smoothly to unravel
All that web of pain
  Wherein ye are holden."

"But brimmed with molten brightness like a star,
  And broad and open as the sea or sky,
The generous heart.   Its kind deeds shine afar,
  And glow in gold in God's great book on high,
And he who does what good he can each day,
Makes *smooth* and green and strews with flowers his way."

" The *way is rough*, and wearying steeps arise;
    And thorns are there to wound our aching feet.
But, oh, those sacred footsteps, firm and wise,
    Which go before ! *they first the roughness meet*,
And briers reach them first !   Oh, shall we dread
To bear His cross — to walk where He hath led ?"

"Indeed we live beneath the sky,
    That great *smooth* Hand of God stretched out
On all His children fatherly,
    To save them from the dread and doubt
Which would be, if, from this low place,
All opened straight up to His face
    Into the grand eternity."

EVENING.

"The day is done, and the darkness
 Falls from the wings of night
As a feather is wafted downward
 From an eagle in his flight.

"And the night shall be filled with music,
 And the cares that infest the day,
Shall *fold* their tents like the Arabs,
 And as silently steal away."

"He most achieves who daily does his best,
 Striving to *smooth* and cheer another's way,
Who, having Faith and Patience in his breast,
 Sits with contentment at the close of day."

WEDNESDAY.

¶ PUT on righteousness, and it clothed me. — *Job xxix. 14.*

He that overcometh, the same shall be clothed in white raiment. — *Rev. iii. 5.*

And to her was granted that she should be arrayed in fine linen, clean and white: for the fine linen is the righteousness of saints. — *Rev. xix. 8.*

Who can find a virtuous woman? for her price is far above rubies. — *Prov. xxxi. 10.*

She seeketh wool, and flax, and worketh willingly with her hands. — *Prov. xxxi. 13.*

She is not afraid of the snow for her household: for all her household are clothed with scarlet. — *Prov. xxxi. 21.*

She maketh herself coverings of tapestry; her clothing is silk and purple. — *Prov. xxxi. 22.*

Strength and honor are her clothing; and she shall rejoice in time to come. — *Prov. xxxi. 25.*

I will greatly rejoice in the Lord, my soul shall be joyful in my God; for he hath clothed me with the garments of salvation, he hath covered me with the robe of righteousness.

— *Isaiah lxi. 10.*

MORNING.

"Thy righteousness, O Christ,
    Alone can cover me;
No righteousness avails
    Save that which is of Thee.

"Thy righteousness alone
    Can *clothe* and beautify;
I wrap it round my soul;
    In this I 'll live and die."

DAY.

"Mine be the *raiment* given of God,
    Wrought of fine linen clean and white,
Fit for the eye of God to see,
    Meet for His home of holy light."

"The woman singeth at her spinning-wheel
A pleasant chant, ballad, or barcarole.
She thinketh of her song, upon the whole,
Far more than of her flax; and yet the reel
Is full, and artfully her fingers feel
With quick adjustment, provident controul,
The lines, too subtly twisted to unroll,
Out to a perfect thread. I hence appeal
To the dear Christian church — that we may do
Our Father's business in these temples mirk,
Thus swift and steadfast, — thus, intent and strong;
While, thus, apart from toil, our souls pursue
Some high, calm, spheric tune, and *prove our work*
The better for the sweetness of our song."

"It is the Father's joy to bless;
    His love provides for me a *dress* —
A robe of spotless righteousness —
    O Lamb of God! in Thee."

"Behold a Royal Bridegroom
  Hath called me for His bride!
I joyfully make ready
  And hasten to His side.
He is a Royal Bridegroom,
  But I am very poor!
Of low estate He chose me
  To show His love the more:
For He hath purchased for me
  Such *goodly rich array*, —
Oh, surely never bridegroom
  Gave gifts like His away.

"When first upon the mountains,
  I, in the vale below,
Beheld Him waiting for me,
  Heard His command to go,
I, poorest in the valley,
  Oh, how could I prepare
To meet His royal presence?
  How could I make me fair?
Ah! in His love He sent me
  A *garment* clean and white:
And promised broidered *raiment*
  All glorious in His sight."

EVENING.

"Put the broidery-frame away,
 For my *sewing* is all done.
The last thread is used to-day,
 And I need not join it on."

"The twilight falls, the night is near,
 I *fold my work* away,
And kneel to One who bends to hear
 The story of the day.

"The old, old story; yet I kneel
 To tell it at Thy call;
And cares grow lighter as I feel
 That Jesus knows them all.

"So here I lay me down to rest,
 As nightly shadows fall,
And lean, confiding, on His breast,
 Who knows and pities all!"

THURSDAY.

THEN they that feared the Lord spake often one to another.
— *Mal. iii. 16.*

Only let your conversation be as it becometh the gospel of Christ. — *Phil. i. 27.*

But I say unto you, That every idle word that men shall speak, they shall give account thereof in the day of judgment.
— *Matt. xii. 36.*

The Lord shall preserve thy going out and thy coming in from this time forth, and even for evermore. — *Psalms cxxi. 8.*

Pure religion and undefiled before God and the Father is this, To visit the fatherless and widows in their affliction.
— *James i. 27.*

To him that ordereth his conversation aright will I show the salvation of God. — *Psalms l. 23.*

And these words, which I command thee this day, shall be in thine heart: And thou shalt teach them diligently unto thy children, and shalt talk of them when thou sittest in thine house, and when thou walkest by the way, and when thou liest down, and when thou risest up. — *Deut. vi. 6, 7.*

MORNING.

"Bear the burden of the present,
    Let the morrow bear its own;
If the morning sky be pleasant,
    Why the coming night bemoan?

"All unseen, the Master walketh
    By the toiling servant's side;
Comfortable words He talketh,
    While His hands uphold and guide."

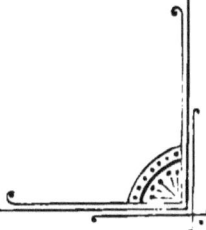

DAY.

"Make me feel
That in the gay and care forgetting crowd
Thou art as near me as in solitude;
Keep Thou the *portal of my lips*, lest words
Of levity, or censure undeserved,
Abuse the freedom of my mirthful hours,
Tinge my each *word* and action with a hue
Of heart born courtesy and holy love!
That in the use of every *social gift*
The happiness of others may be mine;
And every effort which I make to please
May be unmarred by envy or by pride."

"Go and *seek the orphan*, sighing;
Seek the widow in her tears;
As on mercy's pinion flying,
Go dispel their darkest fears.
Seek the stranger, sad and weary,
Pass not on the other side;
Though the task be lone and dreary,
Heed thou not the scorn of pride."

"Go, with manners unassuming,
　　In a meek and quiet way ;
O'er the fallen ne'er presuming,
　　Though thy brother sadly stray.
'T is a Saviour's kind compassion,
　　'T is His righteousness alone,
All unmerited salvation,
　　That around thy path has shone."

———

"Oh ! might we all our lineage prove,
　　Give and forgive, do good and love,
By soft endearments in kind strife,
　　Lightening the load of daily life.

"Then draw we nearer day by day,
　　Each to his brethren, all to God ;
Let the world take us as she may,
　　We must not change our road."

EVENING.

"If we sit down at set of sun,
And count the things that we have done,
And, counting, find
One self-denying act, one *word*
That eased the heart of him who heard;
One glance most kind,
That fell like sunshine where it went,
Then we may count that day well spent.

"But if through all the life-long day
We 've *eased no heart by yea or nay;*
If through it all
We 've done no thing that we can trace,
That brought the sunshine to a face;
No act, most small,
That helped some soul, and nothing cost,
Then count that day as worse than lost."

————

"At evening to myself I say,
My soul, where hast thou gleaned to-day,
Thy labor how bestow'd!
What hast thou *rightly said* or done?
What grace attained, or knowledge won,
In following after God?"

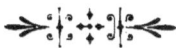

FRIDAY.

LET us cleanse ourselves from all filthiness of the flesh and spirit, perfecting holiness in the fear of God. — *II Cor. vii. 1.*

Wherefore lay apart all filthiness and superfluity of naughtiness. — *James i. 21.*

Not the putting away of the filth of the flesh, but the answer of a good conscience toward God. — *I Peter iii. 21.*

MORNING.

"After long days of storms and showers,
Of sighing winds, and dripping bowers,
How sweet at morn to ope our eyes
On newly '*swept and garnished*' skies!"

DAY.

———

"All may of Thee partake :
  Nothing can be so mean,
  Which, with this tincture (for Thy sake),
  Will not grow bright and clean.

"A servant with this clause
  Makes drudgery divine:
  Who *sweeps* a room, as for Thy laws,
  Makes that and the action fine."

"FIRST ANGEL.

  "Let me approach to breathe away
  This *dust o' the heart* with holy air."

"I have a wonderful Guest,
Who speeds my feet, who moves my hands,
Who strengthens, comforts, guides, commands,
    Whose presence gives me rest.

"He dwells within my soul;
He *swept* away the *filth* and gloom,
He *garnished* fair the empty room,
    And now pervades the whole.

"For aye, by day and night,
He keeps the portal — suffers naught
Defile the temple He has bought,
    And filled with joy and light."

EVENING.

" When in deep silence my expectant heart,
  Waited the sight of its adored guest
  With lamp in hand, I urged a tireless quest
  For soil, or stain ; I sought to place my best
        In every part.

" The lamp-light fell athwart my closèd rooms,
  Like whitest linen gleamed the draperies.
  Oh, fair shall shine each thing that in them is,
  When on my night the Sun of Love shall rise
        To light these glooms!

" Soon with that day my windows were aglow:
  I turned to look my ordered heart within,
  Then drowned my pride in tears ; for what had been
  Pure in my eyes, was dyed with *smut of sin* —
        I kneeled low:

" Lord, not myself, but Thou, must make me clean.
  Let love, a river, flood these *dusty floors ;*
  Write Thy name on the lintels of the doors, —
  Then when again Thy searching sunshine pours,
        I shall be clean."

SATURDAY.

THE righteous eateth to the satisfying of his soul.
— *Prov. xiii. 25.*

For the bread of God is he which cometh down from heaven, and giveth life unto the world. — *John vi. 33.*

And Jesus saith unto them, I am the bread of life: he that cometh to me shall never hunger. — *John vi. 35.*

Jesus saith unto them, My meat is to do the will of him that sent me, and to finish his work. — *John iv. 34.*

Man shall not live by bread alone, but by every word that proceedeth out of the mouth of God. — *Matt. iv. 4.*

And he said unto them, This is that which the Lord hath said, To-morrow is the rest of the holy sabbath unto the Lord: bake that which ye will bake to-day, and seethe that ye will seethe; and that which remaineth over lay up for you to be kept until the morning. — *Ex. xvi. 23.*

MORNING.

"God lives, and lifts his glorious mornings up
  Before the eyes of men, awake at last,
Who put away the *meats* they used to sup.
  And down upon the dust of earth out cast
The dregs remaining of the ancient cup,
  Then turn to wakeful prayer and worthy act."

DAY.

"Only to-day ! dark looms to-morrow —
  Behind, sad yesterdays are lying dead ;
Each moment keeps slow step with sorrow ;
  Give us to-day our *daily bread*, —
    Only to-day !

"We have no strength to walk, unless Thou lead us;
  Sin hides, each side, the straight and narrow way;
Our hungry souls must faint, except *Thou feed us ;*
  Help us, we plead, to live aright to-day, —
    Only to-day ! "

"Day by day the manna fell ;
  O, to learn the lesson well !
Still by constant mercy fed,
  Give us, Lord, our *daily bread.*

"Day by day the promise reads ;
  Daily strength for daily needs ;
Cast foreboding fears away ;
  Take the *manna* of to-day."

"I want such steadfast purpose
  My mission to fulfil,
That it may be my *meat* and drink,
  To do my Father's will."

"Oh, tell me where that country lies,
    A blessed land,
Where without price, the poorest buys
    His fill of milk and wine,
    With raiment white and fine.
    I reach my hand,
And lift my eyes toward that blessed land.

"The King, in beauty there is seen;
    O Heavenly land!
His smile lights all the way between.
    He calls: 'Come *sup with Me,*
    Sweet soul, and I with thee;
    The gate doth stand
Forever open, to the Heavenly land!'

"Then let the King's far highway lead
    O'er sea or shore —
Ye weary feet, press on with speed;
    For I will know no rest,
    Till taken to His breast —
    Forevermore
Safe-housed and *fed* from *fullest, sweetest store.*"

EVENING.

"My hands are weary, laboring, toiling on,
   Day after day for perishable *meat ;*
O city of our God, I fain would rest;
   I sigh to gain thy glorious mercy-seat.

"Patience poor soul! the Saviour's feet were worn;
   The Saviour's heart and hands were weary, too."

"Chafed and worn with worldly care,
   Sweetly, Lord, my heart prepare ;
   Bid this inward tempest cease;
   Jesus, come, and whisper peace !
   Hush the whirlwind of my will,
   With Thyself my spirit fill;
   End in calm this busy week,
   Let the Sabbath gently break !

"Draw the curtain of repose
   While my weary eyelids close;
   Steal my spirit while I rest,
   Give me dreamings pure and blest !
   Raise me with a cheerful heart;
   Holy Ghost, Thyself impart;
   Then the Sabbath-day will be
   Heaven brought down to earth and me."

SUNDAY.

YE shall keep my sabbaths, and reverence my sanctuary; I am the Lord. — *Lev. xix. 30.*

Six days shall work be done: but the seventh day is the sabbath of rest, an holy convocation; ye shall do no work therein: it is the sabbath of the Lord in all your dwellings.—*Lev. xxiii. 3.*

Not forsaking the assembling of ourselves together, as the manner of some is. — *Heb. x. 25.*

There remaineth therefore a rest to the people of God.
—*Heb. iv. 9.*

Let us labour therefore to enter into that rest. — *Heb. iv. 11.*

MORNING.

"Chime on, ye bells! again begin,
And ring the Sabbath morning in.
The laborer's week-day work is done,
The *rest* begun,
Which Christ hath for His people won."

DAY.

"Sundays observe: think, when the bells do chime,
 'T is angels' music; therefore come not late.
 God there deals blessings. If a king did so,
 Who would not haste, nay give, to see the show?"

"I love the day of holy rest,
    When Jesus meets His *gathered saints;*
 Sweet day of all the week the best;
    For its return my spirit pants."

"O day most calm, most bright,
    The fruit of this, the next world's bud,
 The indorsement of supreme delight,
    Writ by a Friend, and with his blood;
 The couch of Time; *Care's balm and bay;*
 The week were dark, but for thy light;
 Thy torch doth show the way.

"The Sundays of man's life,
Threaded together on Time's string,
Make bracelets to adorn the wife
Of the eternal, glorious King.
On Sunday Heaven's gate stands ope;
Blessings are plentiful and rife,
    More plentiful than hope."

———

"Only, O Lord, in thy dear love
    Fit us for perfect *rest* above;
And help us, this and every day,
    To live more nearly as we pray."

———

"And I smiled to think God's greatness flowed around
    our incompleteness, —
        Round our restlessness, His *rest*."

———

"Sunday is the golden clasp that links together the volume
of the week."

EVENING.

"Farewell, sweet Sabbath of the Lord farewell;
Thy sun's last beams are shed on mount and dell,
    And dimly in the West
Day's rosy mantle only may be seen,
While stars gleam out its fluttering folds between:
    Farewell bright day of *rest*.

"To-morrow earthly toils begin once more,
Thy hours of peace, thy hours of prayer are o'er;
    The conflict and the strife.
The joys that tempt, — the griefs so hard to bear,
The rush of business and the weight of care
    Must come to darken life.

"Yet shall remembrance of Thy calm repose
Float round me oft like odors of the rose,
    And peace and rest will come:
A Sabbath peace, e'en in the midst of strife,
A *Sabbath rest* amid the toil of life,
    And make this heart their home.

"Farewell once more — accept my lowly lay
E'en now as passing from the world away
    Thou passest with a smile.
And give me something of thine *own repose*,
And give me strength to bear life's weight of woes
    Yet but a little while."

"And He, at last,
After the weary strife —
After the restless fever we call life —
After the dreariness, the aching pain,
The wayward struggles which have proved in vain,
    After our toils are past —
    Will give us rest at last."

———

"O Thou true Life of all that live,
    Who dost, unmoved, all motion sway,
Who dost the morn and evening give,
    And through its changes guide the day;
Thy light upon our evening pour, —
    So may our souls no sunset see,
But death to us an open door
    To an eternal morning be!"

"O how beautiful that region,
And how fair that heavenly legion,
    Where thus men and angels blend !
Glorious will that city be,
Full of deep tranquillity,
    Light and peace from end to end.
All the happy dwellers there
    Shine in robes of purity,
    Keep the law of charity,
    Bound in firmest unity.
Labor finds them not, nor care;
Ignorance can ne'er perplex,
Nothing tempt them, nothing vex;
Joy and health their fadeless blessing,
Always all good things possessing."

www.ingramcontent.com/pod-product-compliance
Lightning Source LLC
Chambersburg PA
CBHW020254290326

41930CB00039B/1378